I0485234

NOTES TOWARD AN APOCRYPHAL TEXT

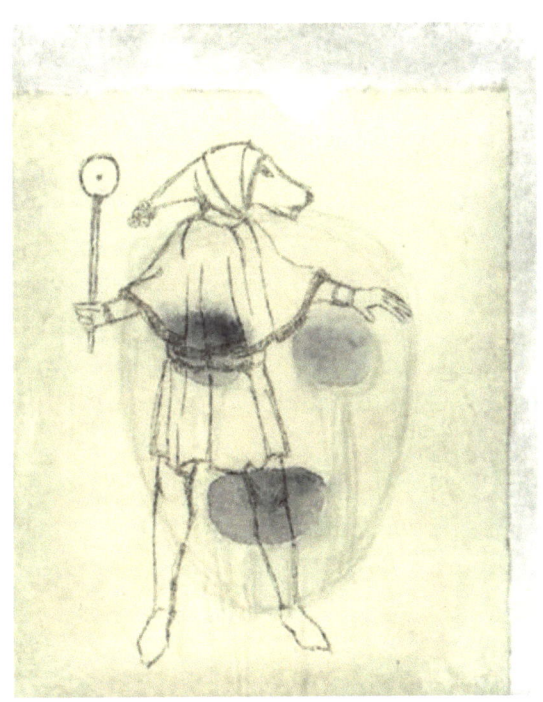

Untitled (mask) 2005

Notes toward an Apocryphal Text:

Poems and Images

Alan May

Tom Wegrzynowski

2014

Notes toward an Apocryphal Text © 2014 by Alan May

Cover, *The Fool Sees All, Knows All,* oil on canvas 48x36 inches, 2010 and all illustrations in this book © 2014 Tom Wegrzynowski

Published by The Chapbook

The poems in this book, with the exception of *El General* and a few others, have been published before in *Perihelion, Interim, Double Room, Willow Springs, Words on Walls, eratio, 9th St. Laboratories, Kulture Vulture, Port Silver, mgv2.0,* and *thicket.* The author would like to thank Rachel Fleming-May, Tim Earley, Sallie Anglin, Joyelle McSweeney, Tom Rabbitt, Jake Berry, Ariana-Sophia Kartsonis, Robin Behn, Hank Lazer, and Tom Wegrzynowski for their help and encouragement.

[*Notes toward an Apocryphal Text*] by Alan May presents a new poet whose vivid imagination expresses itself in brilliant juxtapositions of imagery and language. His work has an immediate power and, beneath its often-absurdiste surface, is rich and haunting."

—Bill Knott, author of *The Unsubscriber*

"Alan May's poems are taut, intense, weird, and occasionally perverse. They are also unbearably kind, consistently funny. This is a poet looking at the world through the wild prism of a broken beer bottle, searching late into the night for the moment of clarity that will set his mad, brilliant, insomniac mind at rest. Rarely will you find poetry that is both absolutely spontaneous and inherently logical, but May manages that dichotomy with deft and surprising turns of phrase, and with a ferocious resistance to the realm of the safe, the expected, the blandly poetic. In short, this is a poet with an uncompromising individuality. Readers who venture into this collection should do so with a high sense of adventure and with a healthy appetite for risk."

—Inman Majors, author of *Wonderdog*

"The poems in [*Notes toward an Apocryphal Text*] are carefully measured, stark and moving. It is a strong and original poetry…"

—Simon Perchik, author of *Hands Collected*

"I want to suggest that the complexity of Wegrzynowski's world creates a fascinating space for theoretical and artistic considerations."

—Brett Levine, Director of the University of Alabama at Birmingham Visual Arts Gallery, from the *5 from 4* exhibition catalog

"Tom Wegrzynowski creates his own ironic mythos, a world in which statements are made specifically to show up the attitudes lying beneath them. His images derive from familiar symbolic structures but refuse to cohere comfortably. What are pyramids doing in No Man's Land? Only Wegrzynowski's symbology can explain, and the explanations may still not satisfy a literalist intellect."

—Jerry Cullum, Senior Editor of *Art Papers* Magazine, from *The First Walker Street Biennial*

"By turns whimsical and dark, [Wegrzynowski's] art channels some of the stark lines and deep tones of early 20th century expressionism, but through a filter that includes flying pigs, armored rats and a squad of masked machinists."

—Dwayne Fatheree, *Tuscaloosa Magazine*, Fall 2006

Table of Contents

I

II

I.

SELF-PORTRAIT WITH LOADED WEAPON

My chair sank in the soft
sod. Behind me stars sank
or slid off the edge of
blue. Down the hill,
rabbits pranced with little
machete dreams. An angry
finch sang a dirge or led a
flock of finches in a dirge.
The laundry on the line:
your little white flags. I
opened a hole in my
throat. A song came forth.
Nonplussed you sat there
in your inky rags. You
sipped your coffee. Turn
the page.

BADLANDS

Adorned in thorns, Ursula
from the aria returned.
The patron saint sat in
silence. He sipped tea
from the conch, muted the
computer. He sifted
through the sand with his
computer. He yawned and
donned a paper hat. She
donned his hat, did a
pirouette in the sand. He
pulled the bills from her
underwear and stuffed
them in the computer.
Ursula returned from the
aria again, balancing an
aria on her stem-like nose.
She thrust her aria into the
air and set it on fire. He
bled sand, cried out.

PAINTING

She's painting my lips a
dull gray and smearing the
line where my jaw should
be. Can't you find a better
subject, says he, while he
levitates the sofa and sings
a German opera. His tenor
is perfect. She smiles
lustily as she paints an
arm pale and delicate as a
dove's wing. I want to tell
her she's getting it wrong.
I think she's falling in
love. She must be getting
it right.

WOMAN SINGING

I left you sleeping I was
drunk and pungent the
church bell rang I took a
walk in the woods the sad
oaks near dawn I thought I
heard a woman singing
was it you with your dark
hair and small white teeth
if I say a word can you
hear me if I kissed your
arms would your chest
swell like wood in water I
was passed out and
dreaming I dreamed you
said something and I woke
ready to respond the light
was on the window was
open in the dark I filled
the tub cut the lights and
drank from the bottle
when I heard you stagger
through the hall and turn
on the radio I saw you in
my mind's eye put on
your shoes and that dress
comb your hair and wish
you were gone

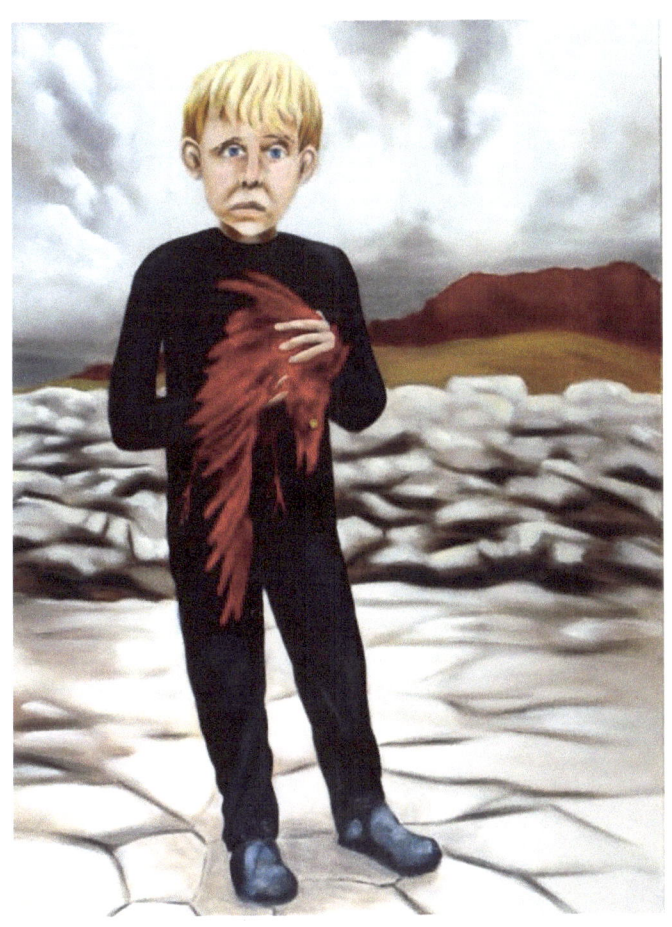

Untitled (boy with bird) 2003

LIGHT COMING
THROUGH THE SHAPE
OF THE MOON

1.

The lantern swung at the
end of its rope the blue
coat floated on the surface
my grandmother's hair in
long white strands I was
nine this is what I
remember spread out like
a fan in the blackness
around her

2.

Her baby in her arms my
sister falls again this time
down the stairs this could
be the solution nip the
sickness in the bud but it's
not that simple have
solutions even entered
Eva's mind my father and
I load mother and child
into the car the hospital is
fifteen miles away the
baby bleeds through my
coat the cuffs of my shirt

3.

One step and
Grandmother flies
laughing down the well in
this dream I fly too above
the strong man lowered
down everyone from miles
around can see his red
shirt and his big red hands
empty now reaching as my
father his brow suddenly
smooth his hair jet black
helps him out onto the
ground I see the blue
fields all around and my
grandmother everywhere
as she sinks flies runs

4.

The squirrels fall furry
bundles from their nests
my brother staggers
stomps one dead
sometimes they are rabid
sometimes they bite my
father hangs way back
behind us in the brush
"Put your gun down
Mack" I yell "I've got to
piss" I don't want to turn
my back to my brother I
don't want to face him
either he might as well be
shooting in the dark he
looks my way says in
disbelief "I'm running out

of shells" "I'm out too" I
lie "Go get some" he says
"Go get them yourself" I
say my father breaks
through the brush Mack
turns aims has the hammer
back "Better hurry" he
says "I'm getting anxious"
my father pale as a dove
says nothing the barrel six
feet from his face I turn
my back and wait for the
shot to open a hole in my
head run all the way home
bring my brother back the
shells

5.

The angel baby flies his
eyes my grandmother's
bright as half dollars we
could buy the world the
angel baby and me the
angel baby sired by an
average man could be a
god he could heal the sick
he could say with his gruff
bass voice: *Move over old
man, I'm taking the wheel*

6.

Fire in the house the mare
runs the length of the
fence my father will say
Mother did it out of
carelessness madness I say
my father and I carry

bucket after bucket from
the well in our drive my
mother is raking out the
walnuts to keep the car
from miring under the
mare runs the length of the
fence while my sister
watches from the yard as
the fire busts out the
kitchen glass the house is
burning the mare runs the
length of the fence the car
is dead my mother spreads
the walnuts with a rake
my father and I carry
bucket after bucket from
the well into the house the
mare runs the length of the
fence turns runs the length
of the fence again

7.

My father is under the
hood of his car from the
yard I hear *Baby, Baby,
Baby* the radio plays my
sister is behind the wheel
Baby, Baby, Baby the
bullfrogs holler my father
prays for help with the car
I pray that our minds will
be eased no help will
come I'm staring at the
moon *Baby, Baby, Baby*
the doctor has said we
should let Eva forget I say
we shouldn't

8.

I find Mack crying in the
woods no apologies are
necessary he gives none
the snow is falling and the
night sky bright suddenly
we are boys again snow in
the south we've no mittens
there is nothing to hunt
nothing left to kill

9.

The angel baby flies into
my room he takes me up
to Heaven we walk around
in the clouds until we find
the ragged outhouse God
in his glory the light
comes through the shape
of the moon the baby calls
God's name starts cursing
and yelling we try to tear
the door from its hinges
God keeps quiet the door
stays locked in Heaven all
we hear are bullfrogs

10.

The angel baby flies
through the church's
stained glass the choir
sings *When the Roll Is
called Up Yonder* the plate
is passed all those quarters

and half dollars Baby's
hundred eyes light the
faces of Eva, Mack, my
mother the choir sings
Baby dips his finger in the
communion he lands on
the pew in front of me
smears the blood across
my cheek

11.

The lantern swings at the
end of its rope in the
blackness   below
Grandmother lies on her
back a smirk on her face
as she sinks ever so slowly
one palm up until all that's
left is the flat of her hand
she is waving no wait

12.

My father and I sit by the
fire and put away a fifth
we've locked the doors the
fire dies down until blue
flames are all that's left
Mack with his shotgun
Mack with his shells all
night we listen to him fire
into the dark

DEAR SIR—

I am like a fish, black
spot—false eye—near my
dorsal fin. Don't know
which end to bite do Ye?

SONG: NO ONE CARES

Verse 1

Not B. Not C. Not D. Not A. Especially not A. And not X, no not X, with her hands lips feet eyes, etc. La. La. La. (chorus: Nor should she.) [note: no other verses]

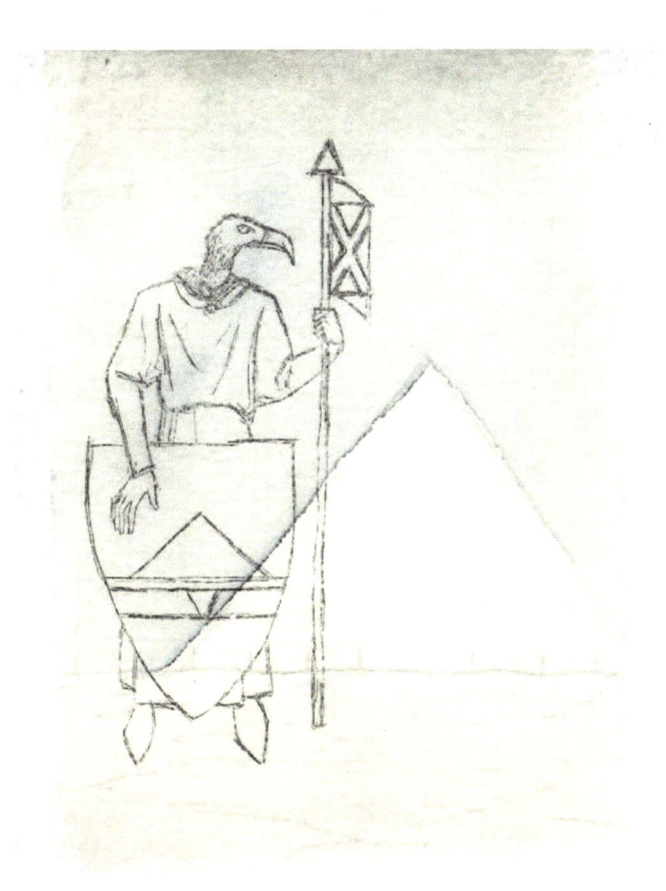

Untitled (pyramid) 2005

LANDSCAPE WITH BURNING ACCORDION

Build a nest, Dear
Elephant, in the elephant
graveyard. Nestle amongst
the tusks impaling air.

*

Don your hat, virginal
shepherd, and grab your
staff. The sheep are off
flocking with the goats.

*

Sir Wolf, you among us
have the grace to howl, to
amass weapons to sell for
drugs and the drugs to
barter with the burning
accordion

*

each chuffed note fanning
the flame that burns the
accordion.

THREE DEAD LETTERS

1. Orphan

In mine, the darkest heart
of hearts, you're the blind
orphan hawking pencils
by the curb. But it's
mambo time. Every
strange body rubbing
against mine leaves me
reeking of a new perfume.
Hubba. Hubba. And look
at you in your sequins;
your new sweetheart with
his alligator tie, his blue
suede, wolf's hide shoes. I
mambo for the door. On
the street, I see the orphan.
Circling the block, a shiny
Yellow Cab. The cabby
guns it, adjusts the
woodblocks under his feet
and the phone books under
his ass. I'm that cabby. All
the better for asking an
orphan to dance. I get out
of the car. I reach for you.
Give me a pencil. Oh,
what beautiful blue rags
you're wearing.

2. Tree

If I look at this tree for more than a moment, I will want to hang myself. Why do they treat me this way? That flower in the corner, the dog's fur, your face? I climb your waist. When I reach your tiny neck, I lose my footing. I fall. I want to chop you down. Your trembling arms. Your buttressed feet. Say something. Look at me.

3. Dog

Like a dog, I pull you through the snow and frozen tundra. While you rest, I build a fire. You bed down next to the fire to write letters to your man who lounges in Miami, who drinks small glasses of white zinfandel; I burrow into the snow. All night I chew on ice. In the morning, one leg hiked, I write you sonnets. While you sleep, the falling snow erases them.

ON A LATE AFTERNOON
IN AUGUST A MAN BEGS
CLEMENCY

His breath uneven he
rounds the corner of the
third floor landing after
having climbed three
flights of stairs his breath
uneven huffing and
puffing he rounds the
corner while the sun sets
in the gray and orange sky
and the sweat rolls down
his back as he rounds the
corner of the third floor
landing the fingernail
moon on his right he
reaches the door the red
door beside which she has
left the trash on the third
floor landing on a
blistering afternoon in
August after three flights
of huffing and puffing he
leaves a rose by the trash
while the clouds float by
drunk on love he rounds
the corner of the landing
reaches the stairwell and
descends

II.

GATHERING THE
HEROES

(1)

I slept soundly on the bed
of dirt and trash in the
parking lot next to the all
night dining car. If not for
the cars parked in neat
rows, the shards of glass
might resemble stars seen
from a grassy knoll. My
Dallas, my W.C., I bled
heroically for you and the
five and dime carousel.

(2)

That Pontiac K-car with
the pool cube in its
exhaust, that was a keeper.
The kitten asleep on the
dash had torn the map to
my dream-child, as if
there could be such a
thing. He carried coal-
lung, he carried pocket
knives, he carried Johnny-
In-A-Bottle. He carried a
small landmine, he carried
books and salt, he sang a
little tune about broken
glass, books, and salt. So
much for nostalgia.

(3)

I was driven in the open
limousine.   I   floated
between the pages of a
book. I ate scrambled eggs
and toast in Dallas, in my
W.C. where the glass was
keen and so were the
peaches. One bite and they
could kill you with their
sweetness and guffaws.

FEBRUARY

So ends abatement the
dying of the stream a child
pisses in the snow snow
that should be dirt to cover
dirty flowers strewn and
left for dead death love's
end a dirty sidewalk
silence nothing stirs not
invisible weeds not birds
and I'm so tanked I can
barely reach the chain to
the light switch so I croon:
If spring makes it I can as
is with the wind cold as
your skin and the sky
bleak and empty as I am
the light dares not touch a
hair on me... my head
curses its luck my cruise
of bitters the only oil for
anointment meanwhile I
shuffle down imaginary
streets where you drop me
like a scraggly kitten
behold I mew while the
darkness pours on me like
milk while the dogged
darkness licks me with its
sloppy tongue

TRACT B: OF THIS
YOUR ANGEL

                       flies
cunningly in night a relief
in arms of relief as such
we sing fallen in this
digress of this smitten
heart still belief of the
train howling into
southern do this play blind
idle beneath raiment the
ditch green grows with
brief life of flowers this
the sick green agent we
know all has been bound
language of amen of this
sickening bloom breath
when with forgotten and
infirm the spirit makes off
like tongue with frenzied
do this: hold to respite and
listen to the blonde rose
flaming petals drape
against our blackness

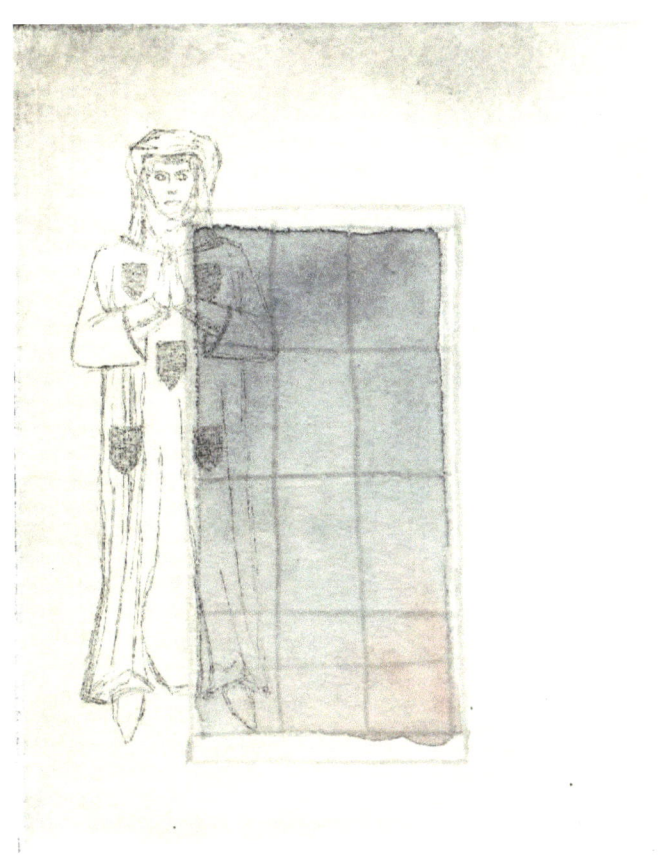

Untitled (window) 2005

EL GENERAL

1.

A brass band gathered
outside my hut, politicos
with long plumes and
matted hair. The queen
touched the blade 'gainst
my cheek, electing me
general and judiciary.

2.

Then came the armadillos
in the armored car. By far
their cigarillos burned
brightest. They placed the
pearl studded pistol on my
thigh, next to cellular
phone and pocketed
politicos.

3.

Orange bands ringed her
arm. She took dictation
from the dictator. The
general hid his disdain for
the populous, their
dyspeptic id.

4.

Locked boxes sought to
tear at my boots. The
bluesman accounted for
my bruised nukes. The
starlight did nothing to
cool me. I vetoed starlight.

5.

The irises and white roses
ringed my grave. The
inscription on my marker
encouraged the uprising.
Each individual crow
returned to its particular
murder, my image
emblazoned across every
breast.

YOUR EMINENCE

Longing for a promised
land, the negated cross
whispered. The great book
opened.   Out fell a leaf
and then a bird and then a
flock of birds. The leaf
was red the color of wine.
The birds sang and then
shot off like missiles.
Your   Eminence,   the
missive of the skull falling
like a pebble into the void.
Your Eminence, I wrote
this   missive   on
aforementioned   leaf—it
floats in the pond into
which the angels pee.

IN REVERENT
NOCTURNE

                                    we
wore broken tongues, we
gazed at the hard bread of
doubt. We angered first a
martyr's bones and then
his ghost. Under so long a
drought,   we sprinkled
blood on the golden calf.
From the Church of Her
Damask Dearest Fallen, a
song swelled with verses
calling down saints. We
drank from the horn of the
birth/virgin, sang the song:
We Followed Here.

BABE IN ARMS

He leapt through the
caesarean and proceeded
to close with the skill of a
seamstress. The
seamstresses applauded.
He kissed his mother on
the cheek and gave the
Haagen-Dazs to the cat.
He reattached the bloody
ear of a soldier. Then, yea
verily, his brother's broad-
sword he lifted and used
as a pointer, while he
babbled in baby coo and
pointed to the ancient text
so readily affixed to the
wall.

JUKEBOX GOTHIC

"Prison Song"

My heart is like a prison
filled with zebras,
songbirds, white mice,
black gypsies, tandem
bicycles, symphonies,
ballerinas, movie stars,
and the world's largest
ball of red ribbon. Oh, my
dear, if only you could
find the key.

"Divorce Song"

My Dear Beloved X, the
alimony check is in the
mail. How's the singular
life? For me it's cake. I
sink. The icing fills the top
of my boots. No bride to
pull me out. Enclosed
please find a father's day
card and a stamp. I send
love to the boys. What
goes around comes
around, or so they say.

"Jesus Saves..."

a dollar for every 100th
sin I commit. He's so rich
He can't fit through the red
hot eye of a Camel non-
filtered.   Love   is
cancerous. It breeds more
love. My heart nigh bursts
for each and every soul.
I'd commit unpardonable
sins to get the lot of you
into heaven. You run, I'll
draw the Devil's fire.

"Ghosting"

I   play   Gary   Cooper's
shadow in *High Noon.* All
I do: stay close follow his
lead. I mimic his dead pan
on the matinee screen of
your TV set. Oh, ye bums
drinking   into   the   early
afternoon, I fill the hollow
of your dread, I add depth
to your art. What good are
lonely   figures   without
their   shadows?   Foil   by
symmetry. On the screen
we live forever, as lasting
as   art   or   love   and   as
present   as   the   stars   we
count   for   each   of   our
distant woes.

"Solitary Girl"

They roll out of town high
in their cabs. Fathers,
brothers, lovers. Our sex is
a cheap motel. The
nirvana they occupy. I
own a television, a ball
bat, a Sunday dress, a box
turtle shut tight for seven
years.

"Drinking Stiff"

apologies to Joe Diffie

Our Dear Despondent
Dirk, Mr. Propped Against
the Jukebox, has
overcome his troubles.
Inebriation leads to
memory loss and a general
hardening of the organs,
the least, the lowliest of
which is the heart. Sir, in
truth we the lovelorn are
here to get pickled. Our
common fear: our
unrequited love will last
forever.

ARTISTS IN HELL

We walk quietly past the
cobra asleep on the
harpsichord. In the kitchen
the robe of the nude falls
from her lovely shoulders,
and her hair she draws
tightly in a bun. The
morning sun bleeds a
horrendous red. The wolf
shreds the lamb with a
mechanism for shredding
lambs. The absinthe flows
abundantly. They've taken
away our paints. So what
of the dark blows of
sleep?

THE IMAGE OF CHRIST

came to her in the form of a shaman who taught her to hang in midair, her arms outspread. The blood trickled down her side. *This is normal,* said the shaman now in the form of Benito Mussolini. The stigmata vanished. *Now you must learn perpetual death and resurrection,* he said. The clock ticked. Due to the exposed wires dripping from her side, she began to contemplate electricity. The shaman took the form of a noodle dish. All ponderance due to the image of Christ soon subsided, though off in the distance, one could hear a moan as a hammer hit a nail.

III.

THE NEW HOUSE

I.

I entered with my new
deck of cheetahs they ran
amuck in the wedding
cake I waited for you with
a glass of wine until the
wine ran out I waited until
my smokes were smoked I
oped a book and every last
word

II.

After several days I began
to relax arranged the
furniture drew on the
walls with my own blood
then I turned on the
television and there you
were breaking bread with
the Dali Lama

III.

Or maybe it was a llama a
fish represents a lion
represents I represented as
I accepted the award I am
represented by the law
firm Dewy Lyle Teatime
represented by this word
and the next tomorrow I
will await your usual show
on the television

IV.

My time in the house drew
close the end of my life
drew nigh I kissed the
imaginary images I placed
my hand on the television
and awaited the cheetah
You running through my
dreams You run among
palms on a white beach
you wave at placid sea
endlessly reflecting

YOU CAN RUMINATE

over the days of well
witching birdsong those
peaches rotting on the
ground or you can face
your twilight all those
stars teasing the blue
horizon they say night is
so much more than we
bargained for

THE SAVIOR AMONG US

He threw bales of hay
from the loft to the lambs
and set the barn bleating
He climbed to the roof a
whooping   crane
descended   and   spirited
Him away text messaging
columns of fire

AXE OF THE APOSTLES

We moved the head of
The Huge Overlord. We
split his sword in half.
We parted the Red Sea for
old time's sake. In lieu of
real apostles, we used
disciples to guard the axe.
They splintered the cross
of Christ. We wept the
faith. We remembered
Thousand. We wrapped
the splinters and sold them
as toothpicks.

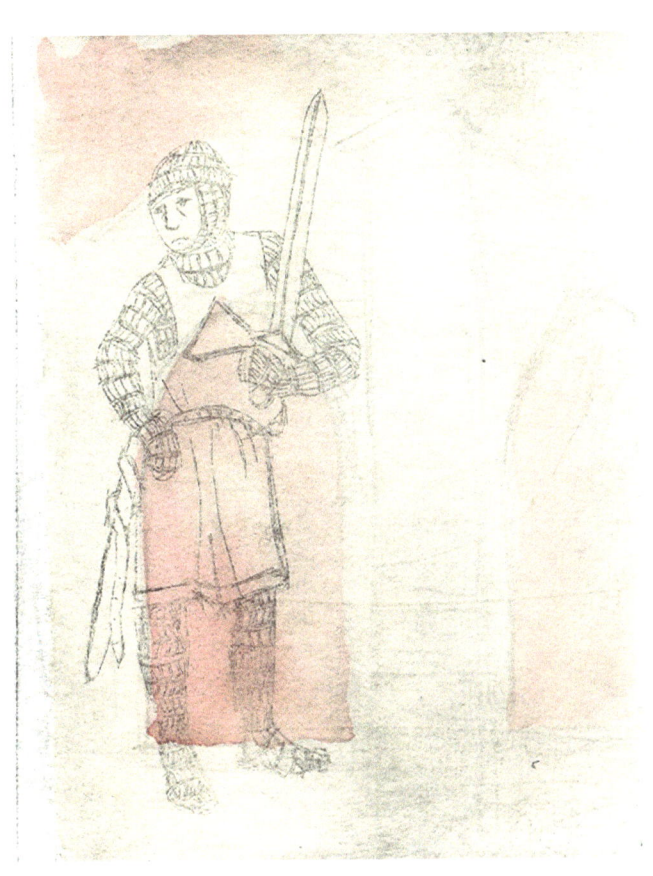

Untitled (ruins) 2005

OH ROCK TO WHICH I CRAWL

In the deep shadows a
depth was attained the
light comprehended not
nor did said light concede
to me I covered myself
with dirt the glass jar on
the hill swayed the stars
swayed the injurious to
persist as stars persist the
splayed tether dangled
from my neck as did my
millstone: the parrot
Absalom Absalom
comprehended the stars he
composed the song which
I sing to you Oh Rock To
Which I Crawl I have
hidden my light within
you I have painted on your
surface my opus
posthumous: "Self-Portrait
with the parrot Absalom"

IN HIDE AND HAIR

I.

To deal with the shifting
snow, Mr. Peacock
became a therapist. His
wrists clotted/clanked.
The skyscraper swayed.
He served his patrons
valentines cut in quarters,
but his patrons preferred
the blind eyes of his
beatific feathers.

II.

Between the cell phone
and the absence of the cell
phone, Lot's wife looked
into the wind and became
the gust that carried
cellular mercy.

III.

The stone lifted like a reed
and clipped Homer on the
ear. Its inscription rose
and slapped him blind. He
chiseled away at the stone.
Thus he eroded the
message.

IV.

Kindness brought out the
wolf in Anna. Her raincoat
hid her eyes but not the
hoary frost in her beard.

V.

Shall I break my pitcher
so that the light of my
torch will blind my
oppressors at the roller
rink?

VI.

If thinking nuclear
thoughts, the horizon
should sprout miniature
madonnas.

VII.

The cicadas chirp to the
grass. The grass never
chirps, nor does that
piercing white eye star
number 1,376.

SONG FOR THE
FRENCH GIRL

1

I know a girl who's
French. Her hair smells
like night.

New as the dew, lovely as
rain, she holds us all in the
strangest of spells.

La, La, La. (chorus: I.
Hate. America)

2

I know a girl who's
French. Her voice a baby
bird's makes us laugh.

She's eaten bread from the
bakeries of Lyon; there's
nothing here but dirt.

La, La, La. (repeat chorus)

3

I know a girl who's
French, shyer than the
moon on a rainy night,
subtle as a star.

Her mouth is a chained
door through which I can
barely see a splinter of
light, a sliver of a room.

La, La, La. (repeat chorus)

BLUE CLOCKS

Oh strange planets at play
in April beat to the time of
my aching head

*

Not   in   the   solitary
obituaries of the day born
of hairshirts and eclipses
examine me in my most
comfortable pose I wear
the pointed hat of the pope
in his chair oh the images
of corsets stropped to the
tongue

*

Not in a place of ancient
negations one in a place of
purple townships (truly
these images induce the
funeral ship) let us remove
the pointed hat and sit
down

Alan May's poems have appeared in *The New Orleans Review, DIAGRAM, Double Room, Phoebe, Interim, BlazeVOX, The Laurel Review, Willow Springs, The Nervous Breakdown, Spell, string of small machines,* and others. His poetry collections include *Dead Letters* (2008) and *More Unknowns* (2014).

Tom Wegrzynowski is a painter living in Tuscaloosa, Alabama. His work is shown nationally, most recently at Contemporary Arts Center in Las Vegas, Armstrong Fine Art Galleries in Savannah, and Transmission Gallery in Oakland. He is also the winner of the 2012 Howard & Michael Goodson and Richard Zoellner Award from the Arts Council of Tuscaloosa. Tom is currently an instructor at the University of Alabama.

www.ingramcontent.com/pod-product-compliance
Lightning Source LLC
Chambersburg PA
CBHW040832180526
45159CB00001B/157